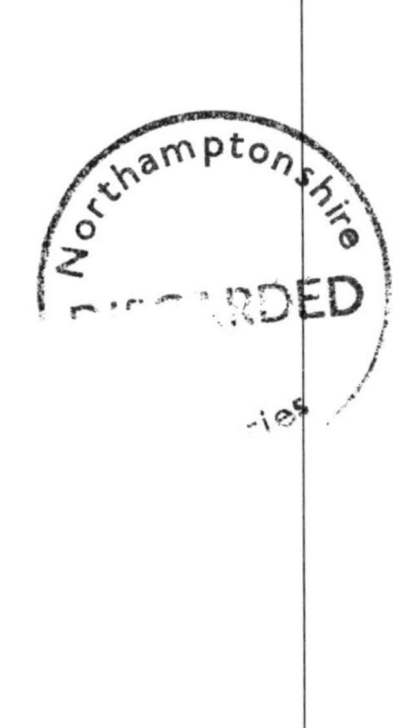

MCALPINE, M.

So you want to work in film and TV?

weblinks

You don't need a computer to use this book. But, for readers who do have access to the Internet, the book provides links to recommended websites which offer additional information and resources on the subject.

You will find weblinks boxes like this on some pages of the book.

> **weblinks**
>
> For more film and tv careers advice, go to www.waylinks.co.uk/series/soyouwant/filmandtv

waylinks.co.uk

To help you find the recommended websites easily and quickly, weblinks are provided on our own website, **waylinks.co.uk.** These take you straight to the relevant websites and save you typing in the Internet address yourself.

Internet safety

- Never give out personal details, which include: your name, address, school, telephone number, email address, password and mobile number.
- Do not respond to messages which make you feel uncomfortable – tell an adult.
- Do not arrange to meet in person someone you have met on the Internet.
- Never send your picture or anything else to an online friend without a parent's or teacher's permission.
- If you see anything that worries you, tell an adult.

A note to adults
Internet use by children should be supervised. We recommend that you install filtering software which blocks unsuitable material.

Website content

The weblinks for this book are checked and updated regularly. However, because of the nature of the Internet, the content of a website may change at any time, or a website may close down without notice. While the Publishers regret any inconvenience this may cause readers, they cannot be responsible for the content of any website other than their own.

So You Want To Work In

Film and TV?

Margaret McAlpine

an imprint of Hodder Children's Books

First published in 2004 by Hodder Wayland,
an imprint of Hodder Children's Books

Editor: Laura Milne
Inside design: Peta Morey
Cover design: Hodder Wayland

British Library Cataloguing Publication Data

McAlpine, Margaret
So you want to work in film and TV?
1.Motion picture industry – Vocational guidance – Juvenile literature
2.Television broadcasting – Vocational guidance – Juvenile literature
I.Title
384.8'023

ISBN 0 7502 4530 1

Printed in China by WKT Company Ltd.

Hodder Children's Books
A division of Hodder Headline Limited
338 Euston Road, London NW1 3BH

Picture Acknowledgements. The publishers would like to thank the following for allowing their pictures to be reproduced in this publication: Eric Robert / Corbis SYGMA 12, 16; Corbis 4, 42, 57, 21, 13, 44, 38, 48, 54, 11, 36; James Leynse / Corbis SABA 28, 27 (top); Tom Wagner / Corbis SABA 33; Steve Starr / Corbis 34; Mark Peterson / Corbis / SABA 8; Tom Stewart / Corbis SABA 5; Peter Aprahamian / Corbis 10; Adam Woolfit / Corbis 22; Richard Radstone / Corbis 9; Helen King / Corbis 43; Ariel Skelley / Corbis 59 (top); John Henley Photography / Corbis 15; Maher Photography / Corbis 23; Pedro Lombardi / Corbis 6; Jason Florio / Corbis 29; Ramin Talaie / Corbis 45; Robbie Jack / Corbis 31; New Sport / Corbis 20; Santan Maria Times / Corbis SYGMA 19 (top); Annie Griffiths Belt / Corbis 30; Jeffery L. Rotman / Corbis 51; Dale O'Dell / Corbis 52; Buddy Mays / Corbis 32; Amana / Corbis Japan 37; JFPI Studios, Inc./ Corbis 40; Jose Luis Pelaez, Inc./ Corbis 41; Tom & Dee Ann McCarthy / Corbis 35; Julian Hirshowitz / Corbis 39; Tom Stewart Photography / Corbis 7, 47; Ricky Doyle / Corbis 55, 56; Tim Page / Corbis 25; Neal Preston / Corbis 59 (bottom); Photex / Corbis 46; Bob Krist / Corbis 53; Paul A. Soulders / Corbis 24; Paul Bennett; Eye Ubiquitous / Corbis 27 (bottom); Roger Ressmeyer / Corbis 14; Kevin Fleming / Corbis 17; Jean Paul Lubliner / Corbis SYGMA 19; Paul Barton / Corbis 49; Larry Williams / Corbis 50; Eric Robert / Corbis SYGMA 12.

Note: Photographs illustrating the 'day in the life of' pages are posed by models.

Contents

Actor	4
Presenter	12
Camera Operator	20
Director	28
Producer	36
Production Designer	44
Special Effects Artist	52
Glossary	60
Further Information	62
Index	64

Words in **bold** can be found in the glossary.

Actor

What is an actor?

Actors are people who take over the role of another character in a dramatic production in a theatre, a film, on television or on the radio.

At one time many film actors had a **contract** with a film company which meant they were paid a regular salary and worked only for that company. Today almost all actors are self-employed and work **freelance** for different companies.

Many actors have **agents** whose job it is to find them work, to sort out contracts, and to agree payment rates.

Many young children have their first taste of drama at school.

Training

Unknown people working their way up from a part in a crowd scene to fame and fortune can happen – but only very rarely. Research shows that today over 80% of actors have had professional training, either at university or drama school.

There is a lot to be learnt at drama school.

Acting is a very unreliable line of work. Most actors have periods of being out of work, which is known politely as 'resting'. Others struggle to earn a living by working in bars and restaurants while chasing after the big break.

Before they are allowed to act in professional productions where they are paid a fixed amount of money to perform, actors need an **Equity** (union) card. These are not easy to gain.

Actors' trade unions introduced the cards to stop the profession being flooded by large numbers of people wanting to act. Their worry was that if this happened, actors would have been forced into accepting very low pay.

weblinks

For tips on the best way to start in TV, go to www.waylinks.co.uk/series/soyouwant/filmandtv

Main tasks of an actor

The performance or recording is only a small part of an **actor's** job. A lot of time is spent preparing for, or taking part in, **auditions**. At an audition actors read or act for a short time, in front of **casting directors**, who then choose the people they want for their production.

Once actors have been given a part, they need to make sure they give the best performance possible.
This involves:

- finding out about the director and other people involved in the production;
- reading other works written by the author of the play or film;
- researching background – for example, if a play or film is set in the 19th century, actors need to find out how people lived at that time.
- learning their lines and attending all relevant **rehearsals**.

Making television commercials is one way for actors to earn money.

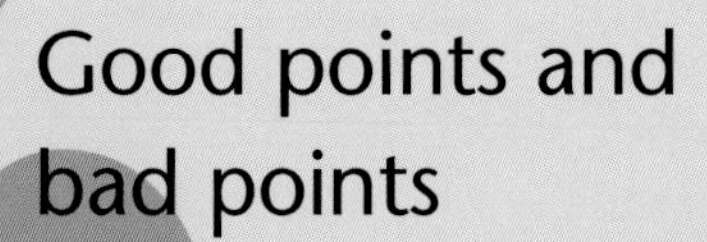

Good points and bad points

'I love acting and can't think of another career I'd enjoy. Ever since I was about eight or nine years old I've taken part in school drama productions and there is nothing to equal the way I feel on stage.'

'Sometimes I do feel low when I haven't had any real work for weeks and I'm spending a fortune travelling to auditions.'

Actors need to be word perfect for rehearsals.

Actors, including those who are well known, often take on jobs related to acting. This can include: voice-over work (reading the background words) or acting in advertisements, recording taped versions of books, or narrating documentary programmes.

Acting work is difficult to find, which means actors can end up doing more than one job at a time. For example, they might have a small part in a television soap at the same time as a small part in a theatrical production.

Skills needed to be an actor

Talent

Talent is important, as **actors** have to be able to put themselves into different roles and convince their audience that they are those characters. They have to be able to control an audience's emotions, making them feel sad or happy, frightened or relaxed.

Determination

Many actors never gain fame or fortune and even those who are successful have usually had their fair share of bad times with little money and no work. Actors need to put their job before everything else in their lives.

Rehearsals can be long and tiring.

Energy

The lives of most actors are far from glamorous. The hours are long and the work for many is not well paid. A typical day can involve a lot of travel and part-time work in bars and restaurants.

Confidence

In order to cope with the obstacles and disappointments they are likely to meet, actors need to believe strongly that they have the talent to achieve success.

Part-time work is necessary for most young actors.

fact file

Children and young people often develop their first interest in drama at school, summer schools, or weekend or afternoon classes.

Most actors study at drama school, or have a degree in drama or a subject such as English, media or communications.

Teamwork
Tantrums and arguments have no part in a production. All members of the team on- and off-stage need to work well together. **Producers** and **directors** avoid actors who are known to be awkward and difficult to work with.

Flexibility
Actors' job opportunities are widened if they can sing and dance as well as act. If they have other talents as well as acting, they can be considered for more jobs, such as musical productions.

weblinks

To find out about the National Youth Theatre of Great Britain, go to www.waylinks.co.uk/series/soyouwant/filmandtv

A day in the life of an actor

James Fermont

James is 26 years old and left drama school three years ago.

7.30 am The alarm goes off and I force myself out of bed. It's not easy because I have a temporary evening job in a nightclub, clearing tables. The pay is bad, but the manager is a friend and prepared to give me temporary work.

8.00 am I read theatre magazines for news of auditions and possible work opportunities.

8.30 am I travel to an **audition** for a part in a stage show. The weather is dreadful, but I keep smiling.

12.00 pm The audition goes well, but there's a lot of talent there. Now I just have to wait and see.

2.30 pm Back home there's a phone message from my **agent.** A television company has come back to her after an audition I did for a soap series.

The series is set in a hospital and the part I went for was a hospital porter.

There is something magical about a theatre for both actors and audience.

The hard work and the struggle for work are worthwhile.

Apparently a new role is coming up for a newly trained nurse, and somebody thought I might be suitable. I try not to get too excited, but my agent certainly seems to feel the soap role is a strong possibility.

4.00 pm A friend who runs a small theatrical group rings, to offer me work at the weekend in a murder mystery evening at a hotel. Murder evenings involve a group of people acting out a murder story, and being questioned by the guests who have to guess who the murderer is. One of his actors has flu and he needs a last minute replacement. I accept and begin to feel my luck is changing.

4.30 pm I read through some more theatre magazines, then relax for the rest of the afternoon, in preparation for my evening shift.

8.30 pm Off to the nightclub to collect a few glasses.

Presenter

What is a presenter?

Presenters work at the front line of television production, introducing and hosting programmes. Presenters work on national, regional and local stations, and satellite channels. Their work includes:

- introducing programmes, giving viewers a brief idea of what to expect;
- hosting certain programmes – children's programmes, talk shows, the news;
- promoting future programmes by talking about them in advance;
- giving news announcements, sporting news.

Presenters have to be well organised and able to deal with the unexpected.

Presenters lead a wide range of different programmes such as **current affairs**, sport, music, cookery, gardening and game shows. Their work includes giving information to viewers, introducing and interviewing guests and making sure the programme flows well and keeps to time. The work of a **presenter** can also involve voice-over introductions to programmes.

Long hours

Presenters often work long hours, including early, late or night shifts. Their basic working week might be 38 hours, but the shift work and unusual hours may mean they work longer. They normally get days off as compensation.

Making guests feel at ease is an important part of a programme host's work.

Presenters often specialise in a certain area of television, for example current affairs (sometimes hosted by a prominent journalist), children's television, or 'reality' television. Some programmes are hosted by famous celebrities, and cooking programmes are often hosted by famous chefs.

Almost none of a presenter's work is done **live** – it is pre-recorded a short time before, and this recording is then **edited**. Presenters work closely with the production team, following detailed instructions, reading from **autocue** or script, and responding positively to any problems or changes.

Main tasks of a presenter

Presenters are responsible for the smooth running of a show. This includes:

- reading background information about guests and preparing questions to ask;
- making sure the various parts of the show run to a set time.

They need to have a personality which reflects their show, for example:

- a pop music show host needs a lively, bright style;
- hosts of a news or **current affairs** programme need to be more formal;

Cookery programmes are always popular.

Good points and bad points

'Working as a presenter on television is great fun. I love meeting people and talking to them about their lives, careers and hobbies.'

'Programmes don't just happen. There is a great deal of work to be done before we go on air. Hosts on breakfast time programmes have to get up at around 3.00 am.'

- children's presenters have to be friendly and energetic, able to talk to viewers as equals.

For some programmes such as cookery, gardening or sport, presenters need to have specialist knowledge of their subject.

Programme hosts either:

- learn a script before a programme;
- read from **autocues** (electronic equipment showing what needs to be said);
- make up their words as they go along.

During recording, as well as talking to the viewers, presenters need to be listening to instructions from the control room and watching signals from the **floor manager**.

Children's presenters have to understand exactly what it is that younger viewers like.

Skills needed to be a presenter

Confidence

Presenters must have a confident manner and an outgoing personality.

Communication

Presenters need excellent communication skills in order to be easily understood by the audience. They also need a clear, pleasant speaking voice.

Friendly

A relaxed, friendly manner is important. Hosts need to make all their guests feel comfortable and at home, if their programme is to attract viewers and be successful. Viewers like to feel that they get on well with hosts, although they have never met them.

Alert

Presenters need quick reactions in order to cope with the unexpected and keep the show going. This means reacting calmly, and dealing tactfully with any unforeseen difficulty.

It can be hard work making sure members of the audience have a chance to speak.

Television quiz shows attract a lot of viewers.

Teamwork
Presenters may be the ones who appear on screen but they work very much as part of a team. A popular programme of any kind is the result of constant strong teamwork with **technicians**, **camera operators**, performers and **producers**.

Technical knowledge
It is important for presenters to have an understanding of the production process.

fact file

There are no fixed routes to a career as a presenter.

Broadcasting is a career in which experience plays a significant role, and you can gain this on college or university radio, local community radio or hospital radio.

Presenters come from many different backgrounds. Some are specialists in an area such as cookery. Others come from an acting background. News announcers are graduates with postgraduate qualifications in journalism.

Anna Costis

Anna Costis hosts a live children's programme. She has a degree in broadcast journalism.

7.30 am I'm up and having breakfast. The show goes out late in the afternoon, but there's a lot to be done before we go on air. The programme is aimed at pre-teens and includes interviews with all sorts of people, competitions, stories and news.

9.00 am I arrive at work. During my journey I've been thinking over ideas for the show and reading a popular children's book. I'm going to interview the author next week, so I need to know what it's about.

9.30 am Team briefing when everyone puts forward ideas and talks about the week's programmes.

11.00 am One of the guests to be interviewed today rings to say her plane has been delayed and she has to cancel.

12.00 pm After an emergency meeting we come up with a replacement for the missing celebrity. It's a short recorded piece, where children talk about their views on homework. However, it needs me to introduce it so I have to think about that.

1.30 pm I've read through today's material and have gone over the script several times. I need to know what questions to ask and be sure of the order of events.

2.00 pm Guests begin to arrive and are introduced to the team and made to feel at home. Some are well known personalities but others are quite young and have never been in a **studio** before, so they need a lot of reassurance.

4.00 pm Recording time – we're on air.

5.30 pm The show went smoothly today without any major hitches. I now have a meeting with the crew about a feature for tomorrow's programme.

6.30 pm I'm on my way home.

Teamwork is essential for a show to succeed.

Presenters are needed to host different types of shows.

Camera Operator

What is a camera operator?

Camera operators record action for the news, feature films, television dramas and documentaries, **commercials** and corporate or business videos.

In recent years there has been a growing use of videotape rather than film, and also of **digital** film and cameras.

Often projects are filmed indoors in a **studio**. In these cases a number of cameras are used, including:

- three to six mounted cameras, which can be moved around the floor;
- portable cameras which are carried around by operators;
- cameras mounted on motorised cranes called '**jibs**', which are used in very high and very low shots.

It takes a huge camera crew to film an important outdoor event.

Photographs

The word 'photograph' comes from two Greek words – *photos* meaning light and *graphein* – to draw. The word was invented by Sir John Herschel in 1839 to describe the method of recording images by the action of light on sensitive material. The first photograph took eight hours to develop.

Pictures from different cameras are fed into a bank of screens or monitors, where a person called the '**vision mixer**' picks out the best ones.

News crews are often made up of a reporter and a camera operator.

Outside events such as the Olympic Games are filmed by outside broadcast teams. To cover these properly, mobile control rooms are set up. A large number of camera operators are employed using tripods and mounts to make sure viewers have a good view of the action.

While major outside broadcast teams can be huge, news teams are often very small, with just one journalist and a single camera operator.

Camera operators are often self-employed and work **freelance**. This means they are hired to work on a single production or series of productions.

Main tasks of a camera operator

Before filming starts, **camera operators** need to read over the script and plan the camera angles, or how they are going to shoot the production. They attend **rehearsals** and practise shooting from the positions they have planned.

During filming, camera operators wear headsets through which they receive instructions from the **director** and the **floor manager.**

It is the operator's job to focus the position of the camera in exactly the right way. When they are not filming they are responsible for making sure their cameras and equipment are in the right place and ready for use.

Senior camera operators are called 'lighting camera operators' in the film industry and 'lighting directors' in television.

Camera operators can't afford to be frightened of heights.

Good points and bad points

'I've had to struggle to become a camera operator, because there is a lot of competition for work.'

'It's important to keep up-to-date with new developments. A lot of work comes from word-of-mouth recommendations, so I have to make sure I do my best work at all times.'

Camera operators need a high level of technical knowledge.

Their work includes:

- discussing the filming with the director and **lighting manager** and deciding on the shots;
- giving advice on how to achieve certain effects.

When filming takes place in a **studio**, the cameras are attached to electric sockets by long cables. It is the job of trainee camera operators to move and untangle these cables. This is called '**cable bashing**'.

Television work is often seen as less creative than film work, with fewer opportunities for exciting shots. However, one area of television work which may be exciting but also dangerous is news camera work. This can involve travelling as part of a very small team to remote trouble spots across the world.

News camera operators need to be multi-skilled. This means they not only operate a camera but also do sound, lighting and maintenance work. In some cases they also edit the film, cutting out sections that are not needed.

weblinks

For more information on being a camera operator, go to www.waylinks.co.uk/series/soyouwant/filmandtv

Skills needed to be a camera operator

Technical knowledge

Camera operators need a great deal of technical knowledge. They have to be able to use different types of equipment including cameras, lenses and filters. As well as operating cameras, they may also be expected to do other jobs such as **sound recording** and **editing** film. This is especially likely when camera operators are working out of the **studio** as part of a news team.

Practical

Successful camera operators are practical people, who can work quickly and confidently in different situations. These include filming among noisy, angry crowds, in bad weather and in brightly lit studios.

Camera operators receive their instructions.

Artistic

They also need to be artistic, because camera operators have to take shots which are not only technically accurate but are also good to look at.

Visually aware

To do their work well, camera operators need a steady hand, good hearing and excellent eyesight. They also need good colour vision, which means they must be able to see all colours clearly and accurately.

Strong characters

Most camera operators are self-employed and work **freelance**, taking different work as it comes along.

Getting the right shot is not always easy.

They need to have strong personalities, and be prepared to work in different places with different groups of people and cope with periods of unemployment.

Friendly

The job involves working closely with groups of people who have only just met each other, so camera operators need to be good team players and enjoy working with other people.

fact file

Many people want to be camera operators, which makes finding a place on a training course difficult. To be successful you need to show that you have a strong interest in camera work through making your own amateur videos, or belonging to a film club.

Camera operators usually have a qualification such as a degree in media production or professional broadcasting.

A day in the life of a camera operator

Helen Ashton

Helen is a freelance camera operator.

6.30 am Today I'm working for a small production company making a television programme about people and their pets. I'm spending the day filming a family of pet lovers.

7.00 am Arrive on location (a family home). I talk to the **director** about the sort of shots that are wanted. I make a few suggestions and then check over the equipment.

7.45 am I set the camera on a **dolly**, a type of trolley, so it can be wheeled around and I can take shots from different angles.

8.30 am Some of the shots will be in the garden. Others will be taken in the house. I talk to the director again about the lighting that will be needed indoors.

9.30 am Shooting starts. It's not easy dealing with animals and there are a lot of re-shoots needed. At one point one of the dogs starts barking, frightening the other animals.

12.30 pm Over a sandwich I discuss the morning's work with the rest of the team, and we decide on some new shots.

1.30 pm I re-arrange the furniture in the living room so I can take some shots of the family with their reptiles. It's a good job I'm not bothered by snakes!

4.00 pm We load the equipment in the van and go back to the **studio** to look at the shots we've taken.

6.00 pm The day's gone well although there's still a lot to be done. Tomorrow we're filming a fish collection so the day should be more peaceful than today.

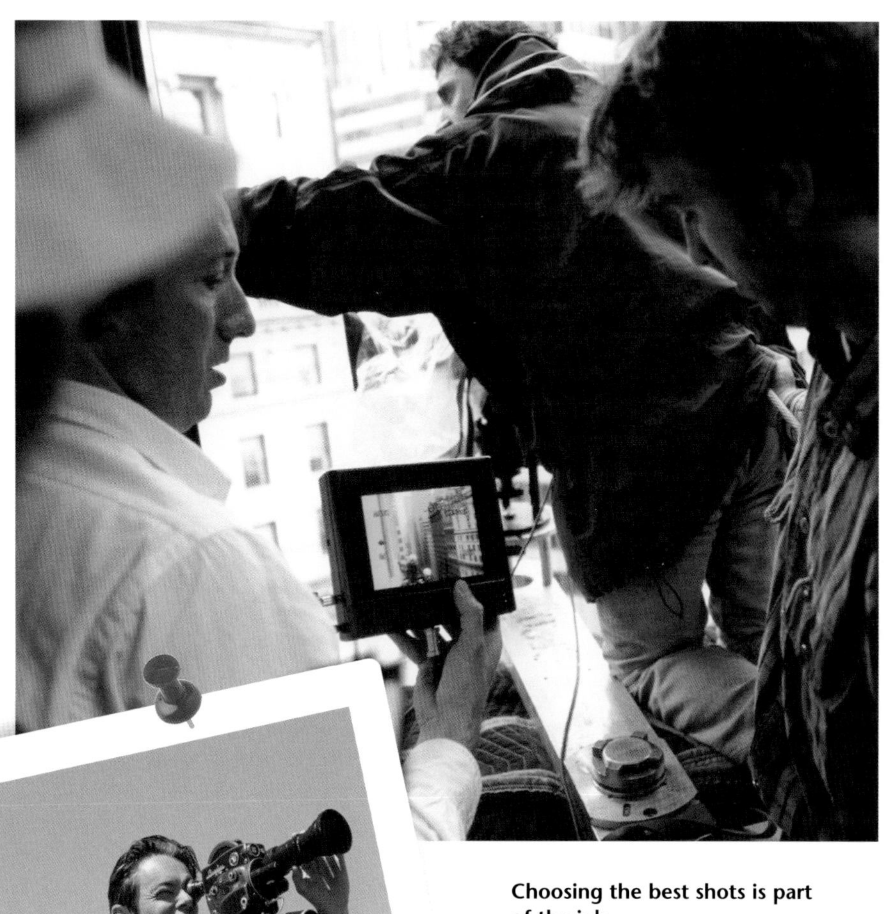

Choosing the best shots is part of the job.

Camera equipment is expensive and must be treated with care.

Director

What is a director?

Directors are the people who have overall creative control of a film, theatre, radio or television production. This includes:

- action
- sets
- **props** (movable objects such as tables and chairs)
- lighting
- costumes
- make-up

Directors work closely with the technical and production crew.

Everybody working in these teams, including camera crew, **actors** and **set designers**, answer to the director. The director brings together all sections of the production and tells people what to do and

Citizen Kane

One of the world's most famous films is *Citizen Kane*, made in 1941. It was the first film to be directed by Orson Welles, who at the time was only 25 years old.

Citizen Kane is important in the history of film making because it used many techniques for the first time on the screen. These included complicated camera movements and flashbacks to earlier actions.

A director's job involves bringing out the best in everyone.

when to do it. If there is a disagreement over how things should be done, the director makes the final decision.

The success of a production lies largely with the director. Whether the project is a low cost performance or a huge blockbuster, directors have to make sure that all the different parts of the production come together for the best possible result.

Although directors are responsible for making the final creative decisions, they do this by working closely with other departments. They discuss the effects that they want with technical and production crews, and actors.

Most directors are **freelance** and hired by producers to work on a particular project.

weblinks

For more information on being a film director, go to www.waylinks.co.uk/series/soyouwant/filmandtv

Main tasks of a director

The first job of a **director** is to read the script carefully. In some cases this will be based on a book. For example, the *Harry Potter* films were adapted from the novels by J.K. Rowling. In other cases the script is written especially for a theatrical or film production.

As directors read scripts they form an idea of how they want characters to be played, the setting, the costumes and the lighting.

The next step is to talk over these ideas with different departments. Sometimes directors change their ideas because of cost, or because somebody else has a better suggestion.

The assistant director checks everyone is where they should be.

Directors are present during **rehearsals**, recording or filming to explain to the cast and the technical team what they want.

In the case of a television or film production, the director's last job each day is to view the **rushes**

Good points and bad points

'My last job was as an assistant director for a six part detective series. This really is exciting and enjoyable work.'

'It's difficult becoming known in the television industry and you have to be prepared to spend your time running around doing whatever people tell you to do.'

Props have to be put in exactly the right position.

(unedited film shot that day). If there are problems with these, a re-take is ordered for the following day.

In a big production such as a feature film, the director heads a team made up of several **assistant directors**, sometimes known as **floor managers**. The first assistant director works closely with the director.

The second and other more senior assistant directors are responsible:

- for the **studio** during recording;
- passing on instructions to sound and camera crew;
- putting **props** in the right place;
- checking exits are kept clear and the studio is a safe place to work in.

More junior assistant directors are responsible for the day-to-day smooth running of the production:

- looking after **actors**;
- making sure people come to rehearsals on time;
- checking actors are dressed and made-up properly.

Skills needed to be a director

Nobody starts their career as a director. It takes experience and talent to work up to this very senior position. To be successful, directors need:

Determination

A lot of people want to work in the industry. It isn't easy working in a world where there is a great deal of competition, with many talented people looking for work.

Imagination

Directors need to be able to form a picture of how the production will look from reading the original script.

Technical skill

In order to give instructions to other members of the team, directors need to understand how cameras and sound equipment work.

Some productions involve long periods of time working on location in different parts of the world.

Acting skill

Directors need to have a good knowledge of acting in order to advise and direct actors. Many directors come from a theatrical or acting background.

Communication skills

Directors need to give clear directions to a large number of people. This includes acting instructions to the cast, lighting and sound directions, and

It is the director who has the final word.

fact file

There is no single route to becoming a director. Talent, hard work, determination and a great deal of luck are more important than qualifications.

Some directors have worked as actors, while others have a degree in a media related subject.

requests for changes to the **set** and **props**. They also need to keep a large amount of information in their heads.

Powers of leadership
Directors bring together a large group of people and make them work together. This means being tactful and patient at times but also being strong, because somebody must have the final word and that is the director.

weblinks

For information on working for the BBC, go to **www.waylinks.co.uk/series/soyouwant/filmandtv**

Sam Birch

Sam is working as an assistant director on a feature film.

8.00 am I'm at the studio ready for the day. The series is shot both in the studio and **on location** in different parts of the country, which makes life interesting.

I check the schedule, making sure I know where and when things are happening.

9.00 am There's quite a lot of paperwork in my job and today I have to arrange accommodation for everyone going on location in a couple of weeks. It's not easy because I need beds for about 50 people in a very small town!

11.30 am I'm given some amended scripts and I have to make sure everyone who needs one is given a copy. I hand over as many as I can and make a note of people who are not on set today, who must receive a copy.

1.30 pm Time to check that everyone is ready for the afternoon shoot in the correct make-up and costumes. I spend a lot of my time ticking off names on lists!

The Oscar Academy Award – success is wonderful when it happens.

Assistant directors have to be organised.

3.30 pm I watch the shooting and deal with any problems or queries that are passed on to me.

4.00 pm There are some changes to the filming schedule for the following week. I type them up, print them out and rush around giving them to people and pinning them on notice boards.

5.30 pm I shall be here for quite a while yet. I need to find a quiet corner and check that I've done all the tasks on my list for the day.

Producer

What is a producer?

Producers have overall responsibility for an entire theatre, film, radio or television project. While the **director** is in charge of the creative side, producers make sure the whole enterprise from the first idea to the promotion of the finished show is a success.

A project falls into three stages all involving the producer:

- **pre-production** – planning;
- **production** – performing, recording and filming;
- **post-production** – editing and marketing.

The role of the producer can vary from production to production. Some producers are involved in all aspects of a production, including the creative side, choosing scripts and selecting actors. Others are concerned more with the business side and leave creative decisions to the director.

Producers spend a lot of time on the phone in the early stages of planning a production.

The Mousetrap

The Mousetrap is the world's longest running play. It is a murder mystery based on the novel by the famous crime writer Agatha Christie, and tells the story of a group of people together in a country house. It has been running in London since 1952 and today is as popular as ever.

Producers have to be prepared to take big financial risks themselves, in order to raise the money to finance projects. If a play is successful it can run for years and make a fortune, but if it is a flop and the show closes after a few weeks, the costs can be enormous. In the same way, a film can make producers a fortune, or result in huge debts.

The producer needs to find financial backing for a project before it can go ahead.

Television drama productions are run in a similar way to theatrical and film productions, with a big team working behind the scenes. Other television programmes such as games shows and documentaries often have a very small team working on them.

Main tasks of a producer

Pre-production

Producers usually have the first idea for a production. This could come from a conversation, a book, or a script. The first step is to find financial backing for the project. In some cases producers are wealthy, and use their own money. Otherwise they need to gain support from wealthy people or organisations, or convince a bank to lend them the money.

The next step is to find writers to work on the script. The producer may have to organise the buying of the rights of a book so it can be made into a film or a play.

The producer finds a director to work on the project and together they select **actors** and **technical crew**. They may use the help of specialist agencies to find the people to work on a production. Producers also draw up lists of possible locations for shooting.

Finding music that sets the right atmosphere for a production is vital.

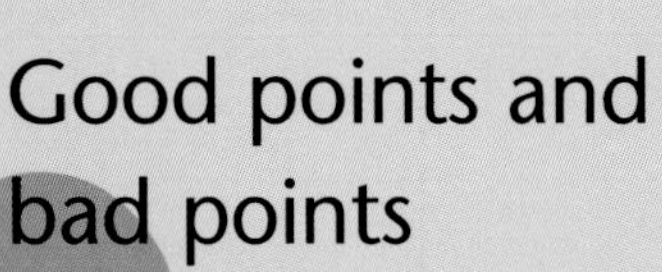

Good points and bad points

'Everybody knows how hard it is to break into the film industry. Especially for those of us who don't have any contacts or famous parents. All too often it's who you know and not what you know that matters. The important thing is to stay positive and believe that talent will be noticed in the end.'

Production
The production period can last for anything from a few hours to months and sometimes years. During this time the producers make sure that:

- all the members of the different teams work together;
- the production keeps to schedule and deadlines are met;
- work remains within **budget**.

Graphic designers work on the screen credits.

Post-production
It is the job of the producer to find:

- editors to work on the final version, cutting and including scenes and making sure the production runs to time;
- composers to write music for the production;
- **graphic artists** to design the introduction and credits.

Producers help to market or promote a production. This means:

- making sure a film is seen in as many cinemas as possible;
- arranging advance **publicity** such as actor interviews.

Skills needed to be a producer

Experience

Producers need to have a wide knowledge of the area in which they are working. This could be film, television, radio or theatre. They need to have a good reputation and a great many contacts if the best people are going to work for them.

Business and financial skills

It costs huge amounts of money to make a film, and organisations such as banks need to trust producers if they are going to support a production with financial loans. Once work is in progress it is the producer's job to keep a close eye on finances.

Knowledge of the market

Producers need to know what sort of entertainment is currently popular, what kind of productions are doing well, and what the public wants to see. Timing is important as the popularity of particular types of entertainment changes quickly.

Producers need to know what is going to be popular with the public.

It's important to find the right person for the job.

fact file

Whatever academic qualifications they possess, trainees often need to prove themselves in practical ways for many years before becoming producers.

Character and experience are the most important qualities, because nobody would consider backing a project without complete trust in the producer.

Calm
Producers have to have a cool head and deal calmly with situations when things go wrong.

Persuasion
Producers need to be able to win people's support and be able to convince them that a project will be a success.

All-rounders
Producers need to be able to turn their hands to anything and to deal with the unexpected. This could include **backers** withdrawing their money, location work running into bad weather or leading actors becoming ill.

weblinks

For lots of ideas and inspiration for working in film and tv, go to **www.waylinks.co.uk/series/soyouwant/filmandtv**

A day in the life of a producer

Shana Gill

Shana has a degree in professional broadcasting and worked part-time for several years producing short films for individuals and companies. At present she is working full-time as a producer of a feature film.

8.00 am A meeting with the **director** of the film. She approached me after she had gained some private funding for the project.

9.30 am At present there is enough money to take us through the **pre-production** and production stages. I am working on finding money for **post-production** work. I spend the morning working through my list of possible contacts, setting up appointments to talk to them about the film and with luck persuade people and organisations to support us.

12.00 pm At the same time as arranging finance I'm working on production, finding film crews, hiring equipment and renting suitable studios.

In the end it's the public who make a production a success.

weblinks

For general advice on working in broadcasting, go to www.waylinks.co.uk/series/soyouwant/filmandtv

Dealing with the unexpected is part of the job.

The days are gone when film companies owned their own equipment and premises. Today everything is hired for a particular production.

3.30 pm I'm just about to sit down and work on a report on my progress so far. The phone rings and I find that the camera crew which I had booked, have a problem with the dates that I need them. I put the report to one side and get back on the phone.

6.00 pm Team meeting with the director and other key people to try and sort out exactly when we'll move on to the production stage. Everyone is looking at me for the answers.

Production Designer

What is a production designer?

Production designers are also known as **set designers** and art designers.

They are responsible for the look or appearance of a production, including:

- the **set** or background scenery;
- the **props** (short for properties – movable objects such as pictures, cushions, rugs and chairs that are used in a production).

Production designers need to have a vivid imagination.

Storyboards

Designers create storyboards or cartoon strips which show the way a film develops and the sets that are involved.

Storyboards for famous films such as *The Lord of the Rings* and *Titanic* have become valuable items, with film fans prepared to pay a great deal of money to own them.

Even very simple sets need a lot of thought and planning.

The work of designers depends on the type of production. They can create:

- a one room set for a television chat or game show;
- several different sets for a theatre production, which can be moved quickly on and off stage;
- a spectacular series of sets such as a medieval castle, a spaceship or an imaginary planet for a film;
- a fantasy set full of colour and glitter for a pop music video.

Designers are involved in **pre-production** and production work. As well as designing the sets and props, they often attend filming or recording sessions to see what is going on and to deal with any problems that come up.

Most production designers are self-employed. They work for themselves as **freelancers** and are contracted to work on a particular project.

weblinks

For a description of a production designer's day at work, go to www.waylinks.co.uk/series/soyouwant/filmandtv

Main tasks of a production designer

Production designers are involved in a production from the very beginning.

- If it is set in the past or in a foreign country, they carry out background research, finding information in libraries, art galleries and from websites. They need to know how people lived in a certain place or time, the sort of homes they had, what they ate, where they worked and how they spent their free time.
- Designers discuss their ideas for the project with **producers** and **directors**, in order to gain a feel for what is wanted.
- When a production is shot on **location**, the production designer visits possible sites with the location team to decide on the best choice.

The first step is to draw a technical sketch of the planned set.

Good points and bad points

'Working in the world of entertainment is exciting, but also very demanding. You meet lots of interesting people and work as part of a team.'

'You have to be prepared to change designs to suit other people, which sometimes means giving up some really good ideas.'

The next step is for designers to draw a **floor plan**, sketching out their ideas and making changes as they go, and then to make a working model. More and more designers use computer design packages for this part of their work.

It is possible to work out the cost of building a set from a scale model.

This is followed by a **storyboard** showing the sets that are involved throughout the film. From this the costs of the designs can be worked out. When the costs are approved, a scale model is made which is used by the lighting, sound and costume teams for their designs.

Production designers give instructions to the workshop about building the set and making sure it is strong enough. Television and film design work needs attention to the smallest detail because of the use of close-up shots.

Skills needed to be a production designer

Good imagination

Production designers need to think of ideas for sets which are original and different and add to the success of a production.

Design skills

They need strong artistic and design skills to bring their ideas to life.

An eye for detail

Audiences are quick to notice something which is out of place, such as a painting or clothes from the wrong period of history.

Business and financial skills

Production designers need to be aware of costs when working on a project. All productions (even very big ones) are run to a strict budget and production directors need to consider how much they have to spend and to keep within this figure.

Practical skills

Production designers supervise the building of the **sets** and to do this they need to understand how sets are constructed. They also need a wide knowledge of different materials in order to choose those that look good, wear well and are reasonably priced.

The production designer supervises the building of the set.

Every single detail needs to be right.

Computer skills
A knowledge of computers is vital because more and more design work is now done on computers with the aid of Computer Aided Design (CAD) programmes.

Team skills
It is important that production designers work well with other people because a production team involves a great many people and nobody works alone. The success of a production can depend on everybody sharing ideas and working together.

fact file

Most production designers have either a first or second degree in a design subject such as theatre design, interior design or 3D design.

Some go straight into theatre design, while others come into the work through studying subjects like architecture.

A day in the life of a production designer

Gina Lawrence

Gina is a production designer. She works freelance and has travelled a great deal with her job.

8.30 am I settle down in front of my computer, waiting for some ideas to fill my head. At present I'm spending quite a lot of time in my studio at home. I'm working on some ideas for a television series. It's about a family living in South Africa in the 1950s. Some of the scenes are to be shot in Africa while other interior scenes will be taken in the **studio.**

I'm spending a lot of time studying the history of the period and looking at photographs, paintings and anything else that gives me an idea of life at the time.

9.30 am A phone call from a friend to say her aunt lived in South Africa for years and has loads of photos and letters. I'm off to see her tomorrow.

12.00 pm A meeting with the **producer,** the **director** and **costume designer** to talk over plans. At the end of it we're exhausted but I think we've come up with some good ideas between us.

The job can involve travelling.

The finished set needs to be correct in every detail.

5.00 pm Final dates have been set for a location visit to South Africa in three weeks. We've also agreed a meeting for the week before, for me to explain the settings I'm looking for.

Afterwards I'm back at my desk looking at some more sketches. These periods of research can go on for a long time but they have to be done if the finished work is to look realistic.

weblinks

For a look at Pinewood Studios, go to www.waylinks.co.uk/series/soyouwant/filmandtv

Special Effects Artist

What is a special effects artist?

At one time **special effects** such as jungle scenes, views of outer space, car chases, volcanoes and hurricanes were not very realistic and sometimes were so bad they were amusing. It was often clear to everybody that the trees were made from cardboard, and walls of houses were so thin that they shook when an actor opened a door.

Today computer imagery has changed the use of special effects completely. Many of these are breathtaking and often a production owes its success to its special effects. People go to see films such as *Star Wars* and *The Lord of the Rings* as much for their fantastic special effects as for the story.

Computer imagery can produce fantastic results.

Titanic

At a cost of about $240 million, *Titanic* is said to be one of the most expensive films ever made. Special effects included an almost life size model of the ship which was built to tilt from side to side. This was shot from different angles as the Titanic sank further into the sea.

Actors sometimes spend many hours having their make-up done.

There are two ways of creating special effect sequences:

- Physical methods – these involve actually building a set in actual size or in a scaled-down version.
- Computerised special effects – scenes or action are created as a computer image.

Another type of special effect is created by **make-up artists**. With clever use of make up, they are able to make a character look older, create fantastic creatures and wounds and injuries.

weblinks

To find out about the work of a special effects studio, go to www.waylinks.co.uk/series/soyouwant/filmandtv

Main tasks of a special effects artist

- **Physical special effects artists** make scaled down models, correct to the smallest detail. They then blow them up, sink them or set fire to them – whatever is needed for the film. Some physical special effects called '**pyrotechnics**' are created by artists who specialise in working with fires and explosives.

- **Computer special effects** artists usually work in the **post-production** period after the film or programme has been shot.

  Computer special effects save production companies a lot of money. For example, they can take shots of a small group of people and paste them together to look like a huge crowd.

Building scale models takes time and patience.

Good points and bad points

'I work as a **make-up artist** on films, television and theatre productions. I'm self-employed and take whatever work comes along, meaning that I work on a great variety of different projects. It's good fun.'

'Some work I do can take a very long time, with the actors being in make-up for several hours. Being on my feet all day can be tiring.'

Physical special effects artists work as part of a team.

Unwanted images such as lamp posts and electricity pylons are removed by computer. Backgrounds can be enhanced or improved by adding sunlight, clouds, lakes, forests or even buildings. Computers are also used to create scenes which would be dangerous to shoot, such as a fight on the top of a building.

- Make-up special effects artists use **prosthetics**, which means they build on changes to the human body. For example, latex or foam rubber are used to build big noses, humped backs or to completely change the shape of a person's face. Make-up artists can use wigs to help an actor take on a different appearance.

They also create realistic wounds using false blood and rubber. Television dramas showing close-up shots of surgical operations in hospitals rely on special effects artists who create dummy bodies which can be cut open to reveal internal organs.

Skills needed to be a special effects artist

All special effects artists need to:

- be creative and have a vivid imagination;
- enjoy solving problems and thinking of different ways of doing things;
- have a lot of patience because the work can be slow and take a great deal of time.

Physical effects artists:

- need to be very skilled at making things with their hands;
- should be aware of safety matters because their work can be very dangerous.

Special effects work can be dangerous.

Pyrotechnics artists who work with fireworks, fires and explosives need to be especially careful. In order to do this type of work, a special licence is needed. To gain one of these, artists have to show that they are aware of the possible dangers and that they will carry out their work sensibly and with care.

Computer special effects artists:

- need to have excellent computer skills and be able to work on a number of design packages.

Make-up artists use false hair and wigs in their work.

Make-up special effects artists:

- not only need to be skilful at creating special effects but need to be gentle in the way they work because they are dealing with human bodies and faces;
- can be working on the same person for hours and so need to be tactful and able to get on with people;
- need to understand the materials they use and the effect these can have on the human body. For example, if some products are left on for a long time they can cause skin problems.

fact file

There is no set route into special effects work. Some physical effects artists come from army backgrounds, some are electricians, some are trained in the use of explosives while others have taken specialist training courses.

Most computer special effects artists have a qualification in information technology.

Make-up special effects artists usually take a theatrical make-up course and then go on to specialise in special effects.

A day in the life of a make-up artist

Jess Morton

Jess is a freelance make-up artist and specialises in special effects work.

8.00 am I collect my equipment and set off for a television commercial. It features two characters from outer space. I've had meetings with the production team and have designs and sketches from which to work.

8.30 am There are two of us working as make-up artists. Luckily we know each other and get on well.

I set out my make-up and make a phone call. There's work coming up for a musical and I want to make sure I'm considered for it.

9.00 am It takes a long time to achieve the right look for the space creatures. After we've finished I take digital photographs from several angles and make notes of what we've done. This is so that if there is a re-shoot, the characters will look exactly the same as today.

10.15 am I check my mobile. The agency recruiting for the musical has left a message and asked me to ring back.

Great news – I've got an interview next week. That gives me time to go through my portfolio (which has information about my career and photographs of my work) and make sure it's up-to-date.

10.30 am We're now on to the rest of the cast who are quite straightforward as they just need a small amount of natural looking make-up.

11.00 am Shooting starts and we're on hand for touching up any make-up.

5.00 pm The end of shooting. I'm needed again tomorrow, but provided today's shots are fine I won't be making-up the monsters again.

Computers are used to create special effects.

Make-up artists need to keep up-to-date with the latest products and methods.

Glossary

actor – person whose job it is to perform a fictional role in a play or film.

agent – person who helps an actor to find work.

architecture – the design and construction of buildings.

assistant director – person who works closely with the director. Responsible for the studio, props and looking after actors. (Sometimes called floor manager.)

auditions – an interview for actors (or musicians etc), when they demonstrate their ability to play a part.

autocue – a device used as a television prompt in which a script is shown on a screen seen only by the speaker or performer.

backer – (in this case, financial backer) – someone who provides money for a project.

budget – the amount of money needed or available for a purpose.

cable bashing – moving and untangling the cables of cameras.

CAD (computer-aided design) – design packages used on computers.

camera operators – people who record the action for television and films.

casting director – the person who selects actors for a play or film.

commercials – advertisements on the radio and television.

computer special effects – scenes or action created by using computers.

contract – a written or spoken agreement.

costume designer – a person who designs (and often makes) costumes for a play, television drama or film.

current affairs – information about recent events.

digital – magnetic tape used to make recordings.

director – the person who has creative control of a film, television, radio or theatre production.

dolly – a small platform on wheels for holding heavy objects, such as film cameras.

edited – the preparing and arranging of material to be broadcast (or published).

equity – a trade union for professional actors.

floor manager (see assistant director)

floor plan – scene plans drawn up before building begins.

freelance – self-employed and hired to work for different companies on particular jobs.

graphic artists – designers who create and manipulate visual images.

jibs – the projecting arm of a crane.

lighting manager – the person in charge of the lighting in a studio, theatre or on location.

live – in broadcasting, material that is transmitted at the time it is happening.

make-up artists – people who use face paints and wigs to change the appearance of actors in a production.

on location – the place where a film or broadcast is made (ie. not in a studio).

physical special effects – the building of models for a film or television set, which are then used in whichever way the film requires (for example, set alight).

portfolio – a set of pieces of creative work put together to show a person's ability to a potential employer.

post-production – the work that goes on once a television or film production has been filmed – the editing, graphic design, etc.

pre-production – the early stages of planning a television or film production – arranging finance, finding a writer, etc.

presenter – people who work at the front line of television production, introducing and hosting programmes.

producers – the person who has overall responsibility for an entire theatre, film, radio or television project.

props – short for properties – a portable object (eg chair) used on the set of a play or film.

prosthetics – pieces of flexible material applied to actors' faces to change their appearance.

publicity – ways of gaining people's attention and telling them about a new film or television programme.

pyrotechnics – a spectacular performance or display, often using fireworks or explosives.

rehearsals – practices of a play.

rushes – the first prints made of a film after a period of shooting.

set – a collection of scenery, stage furniture etc, used for a scene in a play or film.

set designers – the person who designs the set for a play or film.

sound recording – recording of acoustics for a broadcast or musical performance.

special effects artists – the people in a film crew who produce the special effects, either through using physical effects, computers or make-up.

storyboards – a set of drawings representing the shots planned for a film or television production.

studio – a room from which television programmes and films are made, or in which they are recorded.

technical crew – the people responsible for lighting, sound and camera work.

vision mixer – during filming, pictures from different cameras are fed into a bank of screens or monitors, where a person called the 'vision mixer' picks out the best shots to use.

Further Information

So do you still want to work in film and TV?

This book cannot begin to cover all the jobs there are in the industry. For example it doesn't cover sound recording work, animation (making cartoons) or lighting. What it does try to do is give you an idea of what working in the entertainment industry is like.

Reading it you will have discovered that the industry attracts a great many people, so finding a job is not easy. It is an exciting world where people with talent, energy and determination can do well. However if you want a secure nine to five job, it probably isn't for you.

Many people in the entertainment industry work freelance which means they are self-employed and have to find their own work. For some this means times when they work long hours, followed by times with very little work or no work at all.

The only way to know for certain that a career is right for you is to find out for yourself what it involves. Read as much as you can on the subject and try to talk to people who work in entertainment.

Meanwhile, find out about youth drama groups or video and film clubs in your area. You could learn a lot by becoming a member.

If you are at secondary school and seriously interested in a certain career, ask your careers teacher if he or she could arrange for some work experience. In this instance, this would mean spending some time, in a radio or television studio, or a theatre, watching what goes on and how the people working there spend their time.

Books

If you want to find out more about working in film, television, theatre or radio, you will find the following helpful:

Careers in the Theatre, by Jean Richardson, published by Kogan Page, 1998

Getting into Films and Television: How to Spot the Opportunities and Find the Best Way in, by Robert Angell, published by How To Books, 2002

How to Get a Job in Television, by Susan Walls, published by How To Books, 2002

Opportunities in Television and Video Careers, by Shonan Noronha, Contemporary Books, 2003

The Insider Guide to Careers in Broadcasting and the Media, by Karen Holmes, published by Spiro Press, 2000

weblinks

For websites relevant to this book, go to **www.waylinks.co.uk/series/soyouwant/filmandtv**

Useful addresses

Actor

British Actors Equity Association
Guild House
Upper St Martins Lane
London
WC2H 9EG
Tel: 0207 379 6000

Director

Directors Guild of Great Britain
Acorn House
314-320 Grays Inn Road
London
WC1X 8DP
Tel: 0207 278 4343

Producer

The Production Guild of Great Britain
Pinewood Studios
Iver Heath
Bucks
SL0 0NH
Tel: 01753 651767

Special Effects Artist

National Association of Screen Makeup Artists & Hairdressers
68 Sarsfield Road
Perivale
Middlesex
England
UB6 7AG
Tel: 0208 998 7494

Contact the following organisations for more general information on working in film, television, radio and the theatre:

British Broadcasting Corporation (BBC)
BBC Recruitment
PO Box 7000
London
W1A 6GJ
Tel: 0870 333 1330

British Film Institute
21 Stephen Street
London
W1T 1LN
Tel: 0207 255 1444

Commercial Radio Companies Association (CRCA)
77 Shaftesbury Avenue
London
W1D 5DU
Tel: 0207 306 2603

Ft2 Film and Television Freelance Training
4th Floor
Warwick House
9 Warwick Street
London
W1B 5LY
Tel: 0207 734 5141

National Youth Theatre of Great Britain (NYT)
443-445 Holloway Road
London
N7 6LW
Tel: 0207 281 3863

Skillset (The Sector Skills Council for Broadcast, Film, Video and Multimedia)
Prospect House
80-110 New Oxford Street
London
WC1A 1HB
Tel: 0207 520 5757

The BRIT School for Performing Arts & Technology
60 The Crescent
Croydon
CR0 2HN
Tel: 0208 665 5242

The Stage Newspaper Ltd
Stage House
47 Bermondsey Street
London
SE1 3XT
Tel: 0207 403 1818

Index

actor 4-11
agent 4, 10, 11, 38
audition 6, 10
make-up 53-55
publicity 9
rehearsals 7, 6, 8, 22, 30, 31
unions 5
assistant director 30, 31, 34

budget 39, 40, 41, 48

camera operators 20-27, 17
cast 30, 32, 59
Citizen Kane 29
computer special effects artist 54, 56
costumes 28, 30, 34, 47, 50
crew 19, 20, 21, 28, 31, 38

design 28, 39, 44-52, 58
digital film 20
Director 9, 22, 28-35, 42, 43
assistant director 31, 34, 35
casting director 6, 38
creative input 23, 36, 46, 50
production director 44, 48

editing 13, 23, 24, 26, 29, 58

floor manager 15, 22, 31
freelance
actor 4
camera operator 21, 24, 26
director 29
make-up artist 58
production designer 45, 50

graphic artist 39

journalism 17, 18

lighting manager 23
location 26, 32, 34, 38, 41, 46, 51

make-up artist 53, 55, 54, 59, 58

physical effects artist 56
presenters 12-19
producers 9, 17, 29, 36-43
production designers 44-51
props 28, 31, 33, 44, 45
prosthetics 55
pyrotechnics 54

qualifications 9, 17, 25, 33, 41, 57

script *(as used by)*
actors / presenters 13, 15, 18,
camera operators 22
producers / directors 30, 32, 34, 36, 38
set designer 44-51
sound recording 24
special effects artists 52-59
storyboard 45, 47
studio 34, 42, 50
cameras 20, 23, 24, 27
safety 31

technician 17

vision mixer 21